D0460657

LAND OF LIBERTY

AMERICA'S
MONUMENTS

LYNN M. STONE

Rourke

Publishing LLC

Vero Beach, Florida 32964

www.rourkepublishing.com

PHOTO CREDITS: Pages p. 4, 6, 7, 12, 13, 15, 19, 22 © Joseph Sohm/PhotoSpin; pages 9, 16 © Breck Kent; pages 10, 18, 21 © James P. Rowan; cover photo © Lynn M. Stone

Cover Photo: *Carved faces of former American presidents stare from the rocky wall of Mount Rushmore, South Dakota.*

Editor: Frank Sloan

Cover and page design by Nicola Stratford

Library of Congress Cataloging-in-Publication Data

Stone, Lynn M.
  America's monuments / Lynn M. Stone.
     p. cm. — (Land of liberty)
Includes bibliographical references and index.
Summary: Introduces some of the historic monuments located across the United States, including the Washington Monument in Washington, D.C., Mount Rushmore in South Dakota, and the U.S.S. Arizona Memorial in Hawaii.

  ISBN 1-58952-312-1
  1. Monuments—United States—Juvenile literature. 2. Historic sites—United States—Juvenile literature. 3. United States—History, Local—Juvenile literature. [1. Monuments. 2. Historic sites. 3. United States—History, Local.] I. Title.

  E159 .S765 2002
  973--dc21

                                                                    2002004215

Printed in the USA

MP/W

Table of Contents

Since 1884 the Statue of Liberty has greeted millions upon their arrival in the United States.

America's Monuments

America's **monuments** help us remember important people, events, places, and even ideals. Monuments are sometimes called historic landmarks. Probably the most famous monument on American soil is the Statue of Liberty, a gift from France.

Like all monuments, the Statue of Liberty **represents** something greater than itself. "Lady Liberty" at the entrance to New York Harbor reminds everyone who sees her of America's promise of freedom.

The Statue of Liberty was a gift to America from the people of France.

The Washington Monument

Not all American monuments are statues. Monuments can be buildings, stone markers, walkways, walls, or **obelisks.** Obelisks are tall, four-sided pyramids. America's most famous obelisk is the 555-foot- (169-meter-) tall Washington Monument in Washington, D.C.

The Washington Monument in Washington, D.C., is named for George Washington, America's first president and Army commander.

All Kinds of Monuments

A monument can even be just a place. The United States Government owns many "national monuments" that are huge land areas. They are called "monuments" because they mark important places. This book, however, is about historic monuments.

Most villages, towns, and cities in America have monuments of one kind or another. Some are quite simple, like the stone monuments on graves. Others are made with great detail, like soldiers on horses.

The Challenger Memorial in Arlington, Virginia, remembers the crew of the Challenger spacecraft, which exploded in 1986.

This marker at the Little Bighorn Battlefield National Monument (Montana) honors the soldiers who died here in June, 1876.

Busy Sculptors

America's history is rich with battles, wonderful deeds, strong people, and great ideals. American designers and **sculptors** have had much to keep them busy. At least one foreign sculptor was busy, too. Frederic Auguste Bartholdi was French. He designed the Statue of Liberty!

Monuments in Washington, D.C.

Many of America's largest and most important monuments are in Washington, D.C. Washington is the nation's **capital**. Two of the famous landmarks there are the White House and the **Capitol**. The president lives in the White House. The Capitol is where the U.S. Congress meets.

The White House, a famous Washington landmark, is the home of the American president.

The Lincoln Memorial honors President Abraham Lincoln, who freed American slaves with the Emancipation Proclamation in 1863.

The Lincoln **Memorial** in Washington honors President Abraham Lincoln. This marble building has 36 tall columns and a 19-foot- (6-meter-) high statue of a seated President Lincoln.

The Jefferson Memorial in Washington honors Thomas Jefferson. Jefferson was the author of the Declaration of Independence and the nation's third president. The Jefferson Memorial is a round building. Its porch has 12 columns. Inside there is a 19-foot- (6-meter-) tall statue of President Jefferson.

The Jefferson Memorial casts a mirror image on a still night in the nation's capital.

The Vietnam Veterans' Memorial honors Americans who died during the Vietnam War.

War Monuments in Washington, D.C.

Washington has several war monuments. The Vietnam Veterans' Memorial features black granite walls and bronze sculptures. The walls hold the names of more than 50,000 Americans dead or missing.

One of the newest capital monuments is the Korean War Veterans' Memorial. Opened in 1995, it has 19 statues of American soldiers and a Pool of Remembrance.

Hundreds of gravesites and the Tomb of the Unknowns are monuments at Arlington National **Cemetery** in Virginia. They honor Americans who died in wars.

The Tomb of the Unknowns honors America's unidentified war dead.

The Marine Corps War Memorial Sculpture shows Marines raising the American flag on the island of Iwo Jima in February, 1945.

The Marine Corps War Memorial statue is also at Arlington. The monument is a statue based on a famous photograph taken during World War II (1939-45).

Military Monuments

The nation has several military monuments, including Gettysburg National Military Park (Pennsylvania) and the Little Bighorn Battlefield National Monument (Montana). The U.S.S. *Arizona* Memorial in Hawaii is on the site of the battleship sunk by Japanese planes at Pearl Harbor in 1941.

*One of many monuments at Gettysburg, this one honors the
1st New York Light Artillery unit of the Union forces.*

Remembering the Past

The famous sculptures on Mount Rushmore (see book cover) National Memorial are in South Dakota. They show the faces of four American presidents: Jefferson, Lincoln, Washington, and

Theodore Roosevelt. Like other great American monuments, this helps us remember our nation's past.

The U.S. Capitol is the seat of the nation's lawmakers in Washington, D.C.

Glossary

capital (CAP uh tal) – a place that is the seat of government

capitol (CAP uh toll) – a building in which lawmakers meet

cemetery (SEM uh tare ee) – a place where dead people are buried

historic (hiss TOR ick) – of importance in a place's history

memorial (MEM oh ree uhl) – something that helps keep an idea alive

monuments (MON you mentz) – reminders of something notable

obelisk (OB uh lisk) – a pillar that has a pyramid-shaped top

represent (REP ree zent) – to stand for, to be a symbol of

sculptor (SKULP tuhr) – one who carves or forms from solid material works of art

Index

Further Reading

Rau, Dana Meachen. *The Statue of Liberty.* Compass Point Books,
2001.

Rau, Dana Meachen. *Mount Rushmore.* Compass Point Books, 2001

Websites to Visit

National Park Service Cultural Resources at http://www.cr.nps.gov/
U.S. Historical Monuments at
http://ad.doubleclick.net/718288/lPhistory.html

About the Author

Lynn Stone is the author of over 400 children's nonfiction books.
He is a talented natural history photographer as well. Lynn, a
former teacher, travels worldwide to photograph wildlife in its
natural habitat.